*The publication of this book is supported by grants from
the Greenwall Fund of The Academy of American Poets
and the Pennsylvania Council on the Arts.*

QUARRY

PITT POETRY SERIES

Ed Ochester, Editor

Joanna Rawson

QUARRY

UNIVERSITY OF PITTSBURGH PRESS

Published by the University of Pittsburgh Press, Pittsburgh, Pa. 15261
Copyright © 1998, Joanna Rawson
Manufactured in the United States of America
Printed on acid-free paper
10 9 8 7 6 5 4 3 2 1

This book is the winner of the 1997 Associated Writing Programs' award series
in poetry. Associated Writing Programs, a national organization serving over
150 colleges and universities, has its headquarters at George Mason University,
Tallwood House, Mail Stop 1E3, Fairfax, Va. 22030.

Acknowledgments are located at the end of this book.

Library of Congress Cataloging-in-Publication Data
Rawson, Joanna, 1964–
    Quarry / Joanna Rawson.
    p. cm. — (Pitt poetry series)
    "Winner of the 1997 Associated Writing Programs' award series in
poetry"—T.p. verso
    ISBN 0-8229-4081-7 (acid-free paper)
    ISBN 0-8229-5681-0 (pbk. : acid-free paper)
    1. Feminism—Poetry. 2. Women—Poetry. I. Title. II. Series.
PS3568.A87 Q37 1998
    811'.54—ddc21   98-25468

A CIP catalog record for this book is available from the British Library.

TO MY BROTHER, ERIC

CONTENTS

3.

QUARRY

AGAINST ALL REASON

All the locusts stuck to the busted screen
are evacuating their original skins.
If what I'm told of the promised land
is true, it's always
across the border, on a black map
whose nerve endings feel their way across the skinned prairie
to this encampment
where the story being told stalls out
long after the drought has dreamed itself
into dust.
It seems to be August.
It seems the horrid buzzing of things
won't quit.
My first appeal begins *What we did we did*
against all reason . . .
but the apology spills out and sticks
to whatever the riotous ivy keeps climbing like crazy.
On the other side, the riverbed reconciles itself
by vanishing.
By now it's not possible
to get there in a body.
Hard to say if after the wind dies down
this world will revive its wild allurance.
It's the middle passage. The choice isn't ours.
The locusts don't know yet
they're what's being emptied out.

I

WEIGHT

A naked body hangs by its fists from a meathook
rigged to the eaves.

She's wandered up out of the river
tangled in algae and trash, a doughnut wrapper
stuck to her thigh,
a cluster of leeches peeled from her ear,

mouthing the last snatch of some grunge hit
and hosed down in rustwater at the stinking orange trough.

Two strays in a tree.
Two scabbed-up field strays in the poplar screaming
noise that changes nothing,

she hangs there
still, minutes, on industrial chain
from the rotting-out rafters
in perfect composure, rinsed and suspended
as if brought in and skinned.

Other people (parents) laze on lawn chairs, rickety lounges
in swimwear, in the swampy July dusk
tossing back daiquiris from scratch,
picking their blisters, bitching about rashes, itching,
sicko neighbors, whatever,
in-laws, exes.

In a halter dress and sandals, mom
crosses her bronzy legs nicked at the heel,
glares over to her girl, hisses
get down, you
get down from there . . .

Naturally,
the days go crazy around our corporation,
plowing through the inebriate mist off the creek
where busted roses moan.
In the rain gutters, the daubed swabbing of wasp nests
loosen and thud to earth.
Her hands cramp but it's a kind of inertia
keeps her dangling there,
see? The pulse in her neck stutters, blinks, in the television glare
splashing over the sill.

Marsh gas, contagion, tramp down
the far-bank firebush and these eaves sag
under the cumulative weight of ruined shingle,
silt and leafrot run-off,
sixty-odd pounds of unaccessorized flesh and chain,
floodplain of lust, overkill,
stupid echo,

a body feels suddenly light enough to support itself.
Like never before.

Like it never belonged to me.

Someone brings out a plate of leftovers.
Someone rigs the torchposts,
flares them up.

MAP BURNT THROUGH

Of our chosen place,
nothing but instructions toward ending.
Even without desire
the barbed hickory grove ignites upwind.
Mares flee their stalls through crackling mash,
their black figures frothing toward the banks.
Beyond tent poles, beyond the stable's eave, under a gorged sky
reeking snakegrass and clay
that will not, not ever
burst, the silos and shacks in the back lot
suffer the blast in a splattering rust.
Old women thread needles by its light.
Dead ants fry in the wiring.
The crew returns at dawn, blackened.
Two crows in the burnt branches
scatter the roses below with scat.
Their ripped stems spit up a carpet of scarlet.
Suddenly paradise is not ours.
And so we get up and are running
for the annihilated river.
And we are flying for the ruined sky.

BORDER CAMP

One more time I will sit vigil over this city
spine-high on speed—the best available ecstasy
a three-dollar fix.

I will cast onto the moon my lover's face
but it will be the dark head of a crow,
keeping its midnight stint
on a power wire in the night, that screams.
Where have you been?

In flight, over the ore-wrecked mines,
the soot-skinned ghetto where a nation ekes out,
the strip-mined foothills bleeding silver resins in slate,
the huge blossoms of topsoil
unleashed from the baffled land,
the annual empire of ripening hops
crusted with locusts and dust,
the rural shelters still stocked with tin
the season's tenants steal and sell for meat
while the poor war rages

it will scream, as the dark clock ticks,
over the rotted shantytown docks,
the mussel shoals and rust-eaten oars,
the stray dogs faint in the heat,
their fat testicles chewed by flies
children bat with sticks lit at dusk like purgatory torches,

over the lynching ground, black fruits on the limbs,
the stinging salt-flats where the border cuts through—

I have come from exile,
each crack of dawn taming the stars
of their nervous fires behind me,
from the gypsum wind of Sonora
where the ruined fruit is dizzy with worms
and the camps smoke like clouds shot from the sky,
where the thousand stranded and broken wings
wait in the heat for the call—

now that we are illegal.
Now that we are citizens of sand
and the war has no respectable border.

SAMARITAN

No fires in the sky at five, but there's steam
rising from manholes. Trash bags lined at the curbs.
Bronze hydrants.
The upturned eyes of fresh-killed raccoons
glint like coins laid over them.
Stars collect dust in the promised land's attic.

I'm driving toward bread rising for the kilns, my daily living,
driving white knuckle careless
further west into night where the sky is solid pitch.
From daylight, I know these fields strewn gold with hay
mown swift and ripe into bales of sense.

Roadside, two pale horses eat dew in their sleep,
nothing coarse or wild left in them.

I haven't said one word to you since last week.

Up ahead, love,
there's a crumpled panel truck gone awry in the ditch,
its motor still a fit of startled iron and sparks. I confess
the temptation is to roll
in that river of milk
running out the tailpipe—current of detergent and oil.

Then the asphalt dark where the driver's body spilled out.

Then not his face but a sheet taking its shape.

Then medics it is coming closer the red alarm.

Then the deep trees gypsy moths my headlights, horizon.

When I come home
I will not tell you I did this—passing by,
growing smaller than life
because it feels good because it feels.

ECHO OF A SCREAM

David Alfaro Siqueiros, 1896–1974

I understand the rules against touching children wrong.

So I go into the other room and climb onto my lover playing
his silent chords awhile.

No wires, no system, just us in heat uncomplicating each other
as the clock glows.

Certain things happen (engines, stars) during it.

In this age every union is a redemption,
forget politics or need.

Come back in here, switch on the bulb, the fan,
trick shut the shade.

Instinct, as always, relinquishes this body it tends
back toward civilization.

And I think of him sleeping it off
with my face toward this captured acrylic blast,
(war zone, petroleum), think of children touching.
Think of what harm
does the harm we've done do—

In these brushes with death made of alloy and rust,
the child swaddled in bloodcloth
crouches in the posture of lepers.

Her thigh's spoiled, joints
swollen by combustion,
the smoked-out extremities peeled back and stuck
corrupted under blown mufflers
among the trash.

Is this the deadening trade, this pleasure
we issue out against grief? Here on this terrain
of lust and debris . . .

And we are given birth between piss and feces,
spirited flesh caught amid the wreckage.

She screams her shocked body out her head,
that thick industrial assemblage of nostrils and scalp
inconsolable beyond all belief.

We might assume the war is over.

It is nothing now but vicious oil.

(Behind her, a canal's there to sweep the litter away.)

She wanders the heaps, rocking in the fallout, hawking spit,
hairless, hideous, wearing that ancient face
knuckled by panic.

Lay down on this bed of iron.
The profane sticks insoluble to this place.
It is a noise without bounds.

It is you, squatting down, skinned
among the ruins.

DRIVE ALL NIGHT

Away from panic we drive
into the unbelievable heat.

Dust clutches rotted thistle in the ditch
and it's just dusk.

No excess here, like skinning a kill.

Cut the gas but the radio's on soft rock, pop, talk.

Get out so the sky unfurls, white night,
wild night.

Through that static I hear the date 2098 and see another planet,
fictional, guaranteed, like this one

(as if the foothills after that much torched erosion
could still murder or weep, undiminished).

My spine's against the metal hood rocking.
The stars, I'm told, have no remedy but loveliness,
mapping our next destination.

There's dust in the engine, dust in the clock.
Dust in this one prayer manufactured by my body.

Its notes that will not, will not play for me
sound this way.

THE BORDER

Negev Desert, Israel

Leaping from the eucalyptus branch, the wild desert pigs
practice flight,

while salt mines flaunt their electric necklaces—
an empire of runways
for the suicide squads in bedeviled outdated double-wingers,

those sporadic Arab pilots gliding, noiseless,
off the serrated darks bluffs of the valley,

blown to smithereens
by the fixed gunners stashed in secret folds of
sandstone and nightchill.

The moon was a gaping
beckoning eye, a charm on the desert

that caused men to sail the air, silver, wicked,
toward the flat saltplain,

though no one admitted the sea had sunk
back into the planet, leaving a white crescent scar
long as a myth.

What water was left, they could not crash or drown in,
so saline its remains.

They floated
those black motorless birds toward the appointed border
as if already underwater.

By day, we worked the fields—eggplants, dates,
the technological fruits unfolding under veils of plastic.

Beside us their dark-eyed clobbered women
imported over the border on ramshackle buses at dawn,

with spines like roaming slopes
and toddlers flocking their skirt hems,
dirt labor who mumbled in a tongue odd to me,

they suffered the barren clay-hot, late afternoon
hours like soldiers themselves.

We did not dream their dreams—fuselage, petrol, that clutch of fury
that propels the antics of heroism.

I knew even then that by night
they swaddled the bodies of their lovers and sons
in black gauze and hoods

and oiled up the wheels of some discarded creaking glider
for flight.

It aroused suspicion on my part,
like locusts on a rose, spiders on a fresh white wall.

What I knew was the conspiring way
they assailed the air with betel juice spit

and struck with precision
the nail on the sheltershack door,

though no one spoke of it.

WILLOWS

We go by the eddying place in beachwear
to shatter geodes on the common rocks
stuck in the rotting silt off the banks.

Our old man lies on a cot by the willow
kneading his arthritic knuckles.
His skin is infused with the blood of his prize roses.

Every stranger received shelter in my day here
mumbles his dying in shade.
The others nod along, nod off.

Jackpines dream up a shoreline where marsh reeds failed.
Hawks clot the slaughtered ribs of a deer,
inhabiting their heat-warped shadows.

After a few weeks of all the same, the view grows
too jaundiced and common to survive.
At dawn, gypsy moths mount the weeping trunks

to devour their weight in leaves.

FLAMING JUNE

All this talk about drapery and things languishing
out of sheer exhaustion.
Raw thigh, burning muscle.

Carnations wilt off the mantelpiece.
Their blistered petals glow like brands of searing oil.

Her auburn crackling dress is a riptide of fever.

Near her heel, the painter's gauze neck-scarf
half-caught by canvas as he dusted around this
torch of a woman. No doubt she is dreaming herself

into the dark undertow of sienna ocean her hair resembles.

Is our man the painter one who severs the moment
with light—the specter of amber sangria,
Puerto Rico like a pulse, *cezinas* blazing up behind his eyes?

One ear, one heel, her fuse of spine
pared away by brush strokes.
Something so momentary as smoke consumed by his gaze,
it does not exist.

One nipple because it is busy becoming
absolute mystery does not exist.

Isn't she the endurance
of his earliest dream, the one where desire is trapped
then flung out to chance?

Oval table, ambitious violets, 60 watt bare bulb, propped book—

somewhere the century is dashing itself
on the equator, it is drunk
and singing again.

I'm inside this electric fandango of my private gallery,
smoking to the limit.
It's her spoiled thigh that keeps me up suggesting as it does
a century of stupor.
The possible histories her carnations prayed to
have slipped into the distance.

What I want is the moment
retrieved, fully delivered, the tell all the end all, everything

poured into it once yanking free, smoke, spine, dusted away ash,

creaking shadows, scattered eyelash, odor of high season mulch,
undertow—seized, nothing lingering.

What I want is behind you, in the layers behind you, sister,
what I want is not a legacy, not a prisoner, not you

but the dismantled locution of desire.

SUMMER COUNT

A moment ago—this sudden fecundity of just cut hogs.
All the fruit past ripe
lies piled on the ground,
feeding dizzy bees on its mash.
Under the heat lightning blood fills the troughs, and rain
when it rips down the east horizon
smears every footprint in mud.
The last blossoms tear off each limb like heads, yes, caught
screaming down
to strew the matted yard—
a nauseating firmament. An exhaustion.
A *can't catch my breath.*
Tell me, does the spirit grow wiser in time?
Is it ours to teach or us it teaches?
Know shame and whose?
Be harmed or harm? Want company? Make sound? Or
does it stall in motion
as if the name it belongs to were being called out?
That drilling noise—it won't cease—started up as I was praying.
When your calloused hand rapped at the screen
rust on each hinge sang
but in the one wrong key
and the platter of milk by the back stoop for strays
shattered on the walk.
The rain on your hand was enough to carry the storm inside.
When you brushed my hair in the gold circle
on the floor by what fire was left

you said sing to me and the door
let the wind out between gasps.
How can I pray against this noise?
How long before the stench of iron
fades from these palms?
Before the stains dry from these trees?

SELF-PORTRAITS BY FRIDA KAHLO

Blood was her dress and her embassy.
No one suffered with such grace.
She attended her one live exhibit in bed.
They rolled her in with three monkeys
riding the thin canopy. Above
her eyebrow where the third eye
opens and slams like a loose shutter,
her husband the magnificent slob Diego Rivera
and a white medallion skull
trade watch over the crawl space.
Imagine the stamina
of standing for years with that crushed spine
aligned in wire, with vines
oozing from the trap door
in her chest, onto the seething ground,
imagine capturing your own excruciating pose
in oil, fashioning it, flattening it, fastening it
by a hook to your death bed frame.
Which of these agonizing entrances to the interior body
did she find most glamorous?
No one suffered from such eagerness.
She lay all afternoon giving birth
in the gallery, to arrows, scars, to garlands
severed from her stillborn generation.
No one left her altar unharmed.
No one took more pleasure
in the shattered mirror on the ceiling than she.

NO END

1.

I did not intend to pray.
No eye cast down on me.
The smokebushes were still on fire
after the accidental blizzard.

I lay under them, on shore, a long time
down on ash on whose back
petals had just begun the ease
out of blossom. There in no other
disturbance, no other
footprints but mine, the light fingered each black wire
the willows were
in their dead gowns.

In the pond the young ones wore dressings of kelp.
Their bodies never meant to end,
not in this dream, this *in-between*.
And the sky, didn't the sky
look like it could storm?

2.

I woke with a plastic head in my hands.
Put my ear to its ear: static, no birds.

Then I saw it: the mechanism that kept it from seeing—
a past tense of oily prints where a human hand

stitched the eyes with wire.
Then the stillness came in
(it was mine). The shadows in every corner
rang. I did not hear the temples
in my palm humming
but the cavities' terrible frequency.

Then the whiff of petroleum, sirens,
kicking into the middle distance.
Across the valley, citizens
were rounded up and frisked,
a procedure upon the actual body
but there was no emergency.
I am told there is no such thing as an emergency.

3.

After, I switched off the machine.
The oak dock was without finish.
The grain in it rippled, stained with urine.
Light from the south flickered and licked
the ugly planks. *Be not afraid*
cautioned the swans
crossing above the meadow.
In the marsh reeds, in the crickets' affliction,
small gnats hatched between the cracks.
I've followed each instruction given to me
and still each particle
riots.

2

SHARD CAMP

Barefoot in a slip in the midst of all this fervency.
In the long grasses tasseling against chill
aspens shake in the flagrant
din of the century.
Blackbirds blast a downdraft over the grove
like a helicopter squadron from the war
(or a movie about the war).
Women wade to their waists with laundry,
the white nylon garments stick like aquatic mucus
to their thighs. Daylilies blast open,
fleshy, reckless humans.

The kids lay their brains in a row,
in a strip of clearing, you'd think
following some instruction.
No end to bodies scattered all over this place—
pebbles, facts.
There's screaming exhaust
from the junction west of this field, a serpent
of rainwater blowing
marsh gas out its snout to the east.
There's the dream of getting blown away
into the beautiful willows
but instead we roll over and doze
before the call for supper.

Someone's haying upwind, chaff and musk
that sours every breath.

A brief heaving down of things, then.
Long inventions of sage gone wild
choke the back fence.
Is this the temporary allotment?

Igneous shards litter the tarp, flecks of blood
where shattered geodes groan.
In a climate somewhere between gold and strangling,
poor roses resist paradise for a destiny.
(It was the smallest idea left.)

The river is full of rain, the river is
rain.

So many things we must learn while
visiting the new world.

LYING DOWN, WITH HISTORY

1.

The sunstroked crowd moves toward the banks.

Laden with flood-rotted apples.
Oozing wine onto the granite ledge.

The fat swarm of nubile earthworms like dirt-mills,
mud-mills of flesh filtering the impure earth,

clot the choked and holy burial grounds
where ancient ribs
tease the summer of endless rain to
put a body down here, here . . .

The harsh malarial swamps of this west flocked to
suck down into sinkholes—
every suspect in the crowd
with a weapon somewhere on the body.

And the madness smells of lilac, low-level,
chunked out by children's hands clawing clay and roots
in the tangle below.
What will be held against me?

2.

On the petal-scattered trashed grass with limbs akimbo
in panties and one sock, she comes out front.
Sheets whip on the wire lines.

Sprawled in the rough garden
under fresh piles of gravel, under smokestacks,
under headlights approaching, under the rearview gaze
we've crossed every border.

The date trees shake. Ravens nest there for decades.
The night grunts of wild pigs scrounge up chill.
Black points running in spiral, oh—
bats. Bats, disappearing under the bluffs.

3.

The girl crouches behind a slatted fence.
She's blowing apart.
Then a bored yawn.
Get it over with quick.

I sit at the window in nothing
waiting for neighbors to break more glass.
All the flowerheads bloom through nights of rain.
The spirit supposes its shapelessness
necessary to the continuance of this?

As if the dreamer were not us.

And after that?

Sorghum fields black from flooding
leak in the fat heat like sores. Clouds of pests list, stick.
The grove's carved into loungers and stools
soggy from standing dew.

On the first breeze the odor of iron and Tupperware.
We bundle the young ones into pillowcases and carry them.

Is this where extinction carves its cradle in the dirt?
At night the lizards needle their tongues into the damp.

We all lie down in the hush, in general exhaustion
like being owned.

DIPLOMATIC IMPERATIVE

Whatever the opposite of elegy
it must smell like horses and rosewater perfume.

Summer is a levee of talc
the moon rolls around in, at risk.

With such cunning it lights your palm
which makes me lie down at will.

In the elegy of opposites

the odor of seduction and reins in communion
floats in the attic beams two flights up

The rug burns are evident healing, healing evidence.

The window is a lace after shattering—
a mind so touched by deflection it sings.

In the distance the sacrificial epistle of a pistol
or is it dawn breaking?

What we don't know hurts whatever it likes.

Contrary to justice the past holds as much in store as ever.

Shadows double over as if stabbed or laughing.

The wind ambushes a glass of wine,
delivering its proof like another improvised elegy.

Oppose nothing it says and nothing shall make you free.

So I raise one hand to your temple,
a vise grip measuring that pulse in the dark against mine.

Paradox betrays us by solving itself.

AMERICAN INCIDENT

Three years awaiting your next seizure,
a thousand nights out on choking patrol!
At dusk, as bats trail in
from the blue unfathomable beyond
I practice binding your thrashing wings
shut in my arms.
By dark I'm capable as a straitjacket.

In trying to quiet terror
the cash-crop borrows new life from the spoils of last fall's fires,
a slow reparation
civilized by milled lime and bone.
Marsh gas stalks the ruined spurge.
A high summer wind swarms in the fermented rye,
adding a poisonous leaven to its song.

Out of nightfall a woman twice my age
weaves down the ridge,
trying to clap those blasted bats
from her roses. Into the mysterium of sudden rain
you run from the house, naked, and I,
trained only for your death,
don't know what on earth to do.

ORION

There must be a garden under this.
The dam's a bust since Tuesday.

Storm-rammed levees of soil crash
and clot the fields with clay.

The crop roots rot in graves, airblind.

Heat-fat in scarlet the roses' lustrousness
ripens to mash in the back pastures.

Bees swarm dizzy with nausea and lust, a gut
bloated from gorging on sweets.

When they identified your body inside the stench

the needle still hung from your wrist
like a silver thorn.

The muddy firmament, slick with sweat, sickened.
You must know this.

And in your chest the sucked-shut lungs had swelled—

dumb, unirrigated things
there on the floodplain, in the weeds, under stars.

A twister's riddling the horizon like a whale now, wheezing,
a world away.

At night, in the only cool that comes,
I run barefoot along the underwater furrows by pure feel,

shovel the truck from its rut,
drive up the bluffs. Idle. Stop. Kill the noise.

Strip down and fashion a fire from wet junk planks
while the acid kicks in
and dark, Lord, possesses my heavenly body.

Down on the floodplain I can see each
individual hair on each root
float loose from the silt and surface—

a luminous net
dragging the sky's double for stars to suck down and drown.

PHANTOM PAIN

Crazed on cheap rye, we scale the trash-maddened cliff
to the rail lines and crawl
tie by tie the trestle, blind over sheer river mist,
where the trick
is to crouch down and freeze
still as prey while the vitals go numb,
laughing (which feels like
nothing since).
Exposed, irreversible targets in the gold train light
braced to the track where just pure nerves
count, and blood, singing, blood
in the spine, sweat, saliva,
piss rushing down to the black waters,
one long whistle slicing us
at a split second down
to swing, tripped
like stickbombs of tinder
screaming *yes, yes, yes* in the rush . . .
The engine fires by, buckling in speed, sparks, cursing
through sulfur we let
go the ties and fly
freefall into the current—invisible again,
reprieved. Later
we lie flat out in the weeds, in pitch dark,
in wet sand in our skins
slick with kelp, the stars
like animals past burning, the trash fire
between us dying
(but barely).

POLLEN

The daylilies turn white at noon,
orange by dusk. A mother
calls all her children into the basement
and instructs them to stay quiet.
Under the thin veil of muslin gauze,
they lie down in order to sleep.

Night breaks above the soil line,
teasing sweat from the mortar between bricks.
In this dream small white feathers
stick to their hot torsos.
Some suck for air, heaving on the bunks
in drowsy communion
with the odor of oats in their snarled hair.

They could be dead, following instructions,
if not for the creases on their cheeks
the filthy sheets leave.
Some in this room are already starving,
some brilliant in the slant of light through the blind
turn gold, the glare
sticking to their sore eyelids like petals.

On the sill: ice nearly melted through which, later,
stars splinter against the wall. A loose shutter
surrenders. When they told me
to come down here I said

yes. We are a long time by the river
which echoes the repeat of fire from the practice range
on the far bank.

Pollen strains through the fly-specked mesh
printing our cotton underthings with silly yellow stains.
The mother rifles through a pill cabinet.
Where is the prescription?
We are all here,
dispatched down into the earth,
blemished by civilized action.
The noise of our fingernails and hair growing is what
disturbs this day. Our things
scattered across the grove—bread crusts, petals—
pearl in the night heat.

On the drying line imagine the white dresses
lusting for bodies to enter them.
All the stockings tatter with runs in the wind—
bats flocked on a tarnished wire.
It is no easy thing
to be inducted into this mystery—
come down,
under the battered planks, under the urine-stained covers,
and sleep beside the lily roots.

MID-HEAVEN

Four-square poplars on the old weed plat whisper
salvation, no salvation.
Canned goods in their row in the root cellar wait,
wait. The quarry hums.

Crystals sprout inside plain rock in darkness—
craggy and veined (their savant wilderness in secret).

In the small loft over the chapel, wrens nest in thatch.
Deep-funneled batting snatched from mattresses,
hair and raveled thread and plastic they weave
into huts.

We wedge under the corrugated roof
littered by the entrails of small carcasses.

Torched by sunshine, the small bodies we're in
flame up in splinters.
Our mouths murmur in and out of the swaying oak's shadow,
meaning no harm, no harm ever.

DROUGHT, 1970

The girls wait on pine benches,
swabbing their scabby knees with iodine.
Moths whack at the huge bulbs—
throngs of manic wings in one dull buzz.
Blistered skin molts from underthings
on hooks.
Their mothers crowd at the slab of mirror's shattered edge
splotched in black blossoms,
setting pincurls and nets in their acrylic gowns,
readying their bodies for another trip through dust.
Gnats crackle in the electric catchers.
Pollen sifts through the slats.
Beyond the rafters: hollyhocks on the hill, toads, stars
invisible to the common eye.
In the last scrap of heat, in sticky white bedthings,
heaving wet towels into the bins, I swear
they've thought of everything,
if only once, together
in the balmy showerhouse, circa summer, 1970.
Even without glamour, even in this hot vapor
the huge hard-scrubbed nipples
of she who sustained us off her own body
glow, the aureoles
full blown, blood blisters where her nails
stubbed off, her heels calloused in gray rind, each capillary
purple in this scald, angered,

she steps from the stall, she comes up for air, alone,
suddenly in what feels
in this steam, in this particular eternity,
like an eternity.

AFTER THE RIOTS

Los Angeles, 1992

I am released through the anxious gate
into the mob dispersing, and reach through the car window
to startle your body, asleep at the wheel,
awake.

Can't feel my hands, I whisper—their ten identifying inkprints
stick to your mouth, hoarse with dust.

Against Orion
helicopters ride the heat, airing the afterwards.
Trash cans burn all down the cordoned block,
every window shattered where fists whacked to snatch
beautiful loot.

All the way home, no word.
Get: gas, mail, two shots, soap, undressed.
Messages on the answering machine
but the red alert keeps blinking.

When your breath steadies against the white sheets,
I try reaching for solace
but there's none to spare in the customary place.
I try next the oblivion I envy in you
but can't find that firm hold.

(No light, but the moon is still on.)

And I'm lying in nothing against the naked floor shaking,
sucking in nightfog.

Suddenly
God has not handled my body in years,
like an exiled thing.

Forever comes to mind in the long time it takes
for the last trash pyres to perish into ash.
The whore a story beneath us begins to finish him,
uttering one word over his choked groin with such tenderness
I too am soothed.

Two animals, I don't know what kind,
keen in the dark garden until dawn.

ON REFLECTION

In the film adaptation of Chekhov's *Platonov*
half the family is brained on madeira
before the opening credits.
When others arrive, hauling more booze,
the conversation smears
across the screen, an oozing wound.
By noon, no character remembers exactly why
they've come. Like swollen riverbeds
they lay their astounded selves down,
stunned, while out in the courtyard,
in the reflecting shade, a mechanical piano
keeps spinning the cast
into stupor. In a minor key,
they sit at the banquet table
drowned: dreaming
of music.

Suppose it's this heat
that mires the whole ugly mess of our coupling.
The mirror—the last prop that's any fun—
fogs over, wept at, sweated on,
the dark's got drunk on the soiled rug
in the thick of this Slavic sleep
silvering in static while our soundtrack waltzes on,
no one at the keyboard, no one awake enough
to rip out the script,
everyone's misery sick but still breathing, dumb

but every heart still
bleeding, doubled over
and over again
in our own likenesses—

EMERGENCY

If that siren were coming for me
I'd be flat out on the mattress taking vows
to fill my life with bells and the miracles of sand,
given the prospect of dying before my time.

If that wind were meant for me
I'd order it to come in closer
with a few wet leaves for the added touch,
no more ideas of comfort in ideas—

no more comfort in stillborn meadows.

If that lightning flash were coming for me
I'd take this gold moment by the throat
and climb onto the rooftop to begin again,
honest as a bounty of rain.

No more lying out of shame or pity.
No more lying for no reason at all.

I'd rent a window in a foreign border town
with cliffs in view and linden trees for shade.
I'd greet strangers with an open face.
I'd dance nightly in that sky of fire.
I'd wade hip-deep in rubythrush and mist, and hell
I'd blindfold my theories and let them feel
their way home.

QUARRY

We went to the ditches. We went to the palace.
Went to the jungle-choked pyramid, the seven mosques.
To the chambers carved from the bowels of grottoes.
The coliseum the museum the marketplace under sun-stained silk.
Bunks and showers, laboratory and cockpit, slum
called city of sun, field called hell of cotton.
We went to the napalm-slashed swatches, into the claw-carved
        quarry
listening for the epic
trail off into whispers, and always

back to this the river reeking vinegar and rye we come
in, all the way in
and rinse and, if there's enough time, if there's enough water,
rinse again.

3

HOW STRANGE AND FINE
TO GET SO NEAR TO IT

From a line in the poem "Finding Something" by Jack Gilbert

We sit on the back stoop eating noodles and broth.
The children next door make of their naked bodies
a joyous occasion in the rain turning to hail.
Aglow in white lightning,
how close to the center of the storm
they play, their laughter
stealing into the beds beneath us,
whacking tops off the gorgeous roses
before even blooming.
In slow motion: the alley chokes in ice the size of figs.
In barely what light's left
they scatter about the slick asphalt,
carrying the small sweet-meated heads of carpsuckers
their uncles snagged off the cargo-yard docks.
Steaming, they scavenge
the industrial Dumpsters for junk
from the crackhouse raid—
hubcaps, coils berserking loose in heaps of ripped shag,
frilly lampshades for skirts.
It all reeks of sweat and grease, liquor, rust.
Under the power lines the unharmed children
shriek through the silvering sleet.
The grandmother crouches in exile
on the walk, five impossibly small pairs of
bleached underpants stacked in her fat lap.
Nothing by now shames her.

Beneath her soaked robe the ribs ripple
like a stone's been thrown in her heart and sunk.
They surface from the garbage bins for air,
shouting *fuck you, fuck you* into the new world
with such absurd laughter
even we agree. Great weather, great soup,
great trash of fine things.
Their small swearing bodies bruised by the hail
begin to blue like jewels.

THE NEWS

So I took notes on the skin of the burned girl
stained with gasoline.
The exploded brain of the man sucking off an exhaust pipe.
The drunk crow whose every orifice
was entered by the beam of a hand-held light
last night in a filthy alley.
I turned on the machine. Listen,
it started to hum static.
Did you run for the river?
Does an idea smear at that speed?
Were you already in flight when the metal
contraption slipped under your wings?
I said speak up for the recorder.
Speak right into it or your voice is just noise.
I said to the man with a black hole in his mind
let's go back to the torture part.
You swear there was not food or air enough.
That the shackle healing into your ankle
was in fact invisible?
And that later a knife was needed
to cut free?
Yes, but the river was dry.
Time looks almost holy smearing.
And these wings were never designed for flight.
I said tell in your own words
what it felt like.
Like being skinned.
Falling out of the sun.
A knife.

ALIBI

We smoke in the TV's static, after prime time,
while your body-double climbs from its sunken gold cage

shouting laws neither of us is willing to obey—
not with this manic piano sonata in play, not given all

our making out in the panic the salt mist and moonlight shatters
across this bed, this fractured appetite

no time or amount of heavy petting can cure.
I'm just lip synching the voice-over.

The urge storms me to dial up and order desire
delivered, quick—anything's a revolution when the whole globe's
    mapped.

Outside the ice weeps willows and dawn's early light
fires the opening salvo of what will be

another setting up of base camp in God's blind spot.
I don't want to talk about the greater pleasures

and who even asked? I don't
want what lies go with them, only the evident adage

that whatever gives us birth burns.
Could be an elegy, could be an anthem, whatever else

the strictly ornamental grass sticking up through the blown drifts is
it's functioning beautifully against the wind,

and that figure mottled by night sweats is fastening itself
back into the ambient fit of your body.

Maybe I should flee the scene of this accident.
If they track me down later, what should I say

I am to you?
They'll all want to know.

WHITE NIGHTS

For my father, in St. Petersburg

All afternoon in a kind of exile
he has sat under the iron lamps of the archive
arguing into one tongue from another
the memoirs of Lenin's attorney during the first harsh trials.
This is his solitary confinement—
lifting the remedial defense from dead pages
as if the thought of resurrection has not been lost
but simply lost its body.

Now, on this brown earth, I imagine the man a stranger to me,
though his hands cramped numb from work
brushed a childhood through his daughter's hair
snarled all dusk in hard play.
I have heard him on occasion sink down
and beg forgiveness from his God
for all ignorance in raising to life a child
who charges through the stunned inebriate days,
unmoored.

In the afterward now, he is free—
here in the anonymous open of the park, sundown,
not a soul around to ask what he doesn't know,
only directions, the hour please, the word
in his language to mean *stars*.
A sentry turns and greets his nod,
disregarding a moment the issue of weapons.

Burnt ivy weaves to the fountain brink,
changing it.

It should be easier now
to imagine the statue's extremities
shorn off by seasons of freezing and ice,
but I still don't know when time
stops belonging to us,
or us to it.
There by the fountain he appears lost
in a pleasure I haven't known in years,
scissoring the sun in waves
from his girl's neck.

But it is the music that carries him off,
spilling from a window like a tide come in
as his exhausted body cuts
through the rain silvering the dark
where a student—she must be just learning—
begins her nightly recital,
afloat, *andante*, helping the instrument
release its haunted score.

GOLDEN RULE

I have a daughter whose mind is cruel.
Every spring she asks me
Will you cut my hair
straight and clean like it was before?

I confess weakness.
I confess to a sadness so whole and thorough
even her words are a stranger's.

Who in their right mind
wouldn't want pity, now in the gold light
of April? I have a daughter
whose mind is cruel.

Snow's blown into a bias along the fence:
it can go no further.
Who at the sight of it, who but me,
wouldn't turn around and stare down his own?
I'm lost for the word.

When I feel it rising
I rise to make the cut,
another year's growth, brown and split.

I wrap a damp towel around her neck.

My hands know nothing but the feel of it.

She is wearing my favorite dress.

SEE UNDER:

There's a word for a beggar who fakes being blind.
Another for amnesia about all events underwater.
For the exact center of gravity in a skyscraper.
Without motive, a bullet whittled from ice
utters murder into a toddler's chest.
The sun makes a pool of water around her body
that will evaporate by noon, a shadow
advertising the precise time of death.
There's a word for a cannon fired from a camel's back.
Another for a rain gauge fueled by the sun.
For anything that lasts all night.
The rumor of a violent stormfront
keeps arriving,
but somewhere else.

SHUTTLE

Look—it's her (the woman you've waited on)
come back from the open market.

The alley as she heads down it now
is a pattern of ruts and collapses leading to your door.

The injuries happened slowly, under pretense of travel.

Isn't that how she's come, injured herself, spent,
the cost of this latest chaos in her arms?

It's too late to stop
the blue screen from glowing, or the alarm of it

glowing, it's way past launching the exploding
hand of salt, ash of the bodies.

When the capsule blazed in on itself,
all measurement began again, a crease.

The passengers in numbered bunks
fell off the other edge.

She knocks, she wants help with that load.

What more than the already deadweight is there
to give, more flesh, more devotion?

Talk first of the snow lilies by the walk.
Talk of airstrips, talk of the text you've been reading:

in which the exiled settlement
goes extinct by the riverbank.

Things have shattered into the afterwards.
She moves her attention into it

as if you never did matter.

One moment she's entering the door you hold open
and the next she can't remember

whose hand is doing the helping.

Is hers a face you still know
and would swear by?

Has she let go your hand
for fear of turning you to ash?

And all you feel is the bruise

the shape of her face, the size of a planet.

THE AND OF ONE

I got up and left your lovemaking by ambulance
In the hallway I crawled past the illuminated roses
You came at me in that grimy sheet
With my smell glued in the creases and those creases
In turn in my cheek after sleep
Against which the wall whispered *go*
And I went for the stairs I went down on all fours
Sideways as if into a shaft cored into gold
That impossible light just after fainting
A shaft licked by pollen, incandescent hole
With a dumb chapel in the pit of its guts
Where I knew there was no word, no curse or reply
You could shout into that pit to save me

MOMENT'S NOTICE

1.

To it as to a reprieve I come
and kick back into the bus's cruising noises—
a full allotment of rapture.

Even intelligence has its reckless harbors,
spoils in the rock, illegal features,
blow-holes ripped open and swollen

like a quarrel corrupting
that otherwise constant tide, the ideal, ordained.

2.

My first instinct is painting. In which motion
brushes up against fate.

Torment, over the succession of days, of ages, glazed
into a captive, battened still life—a past living.

So that unlike life, nothing might go wrong again.
No risks run further through the gears,
irritations calm, even in Breughel's favorite topic

which is oblivion as a formal pursuit.

Dark strokes the coast in blind surveillance.
The crowd works itself flush over the terrestrial deck.
They, the load, bound to everyday keel and swell,

caught up in purpose—caught in the act—as one
clamoring allegiance to course.

See how they train toward the amnesia
faith in tradition creates?

The sky is smaller than in earlier scenes,
bled into by the imperialized, mundane life they lead
like a beast hauling goods to barter.

Density, meanwhile, sucks the marginal subject
back into the thick, shot down, wounded,
just in time to be missed—though
this failure too is right,

given the lapse, the fugue, the crowd's paralysis,
all past drained of use.

Our sometime dreamer
enters sails and all the vast unseen,
though he never quite makes it before
the finishing touch.

This is the medium's genius: nothing that matters escapes.
Therefore I will be quiet, comforted that I am dust.

3.

Lost in my last thought, the evening bus—
steered up the crest by a vet still dressed in fatigues
for some imagined mission—shakes

like embodied applause to a halt
deep in the overpass where no lights work.

What goes wrong is a cork in a port bottle in back blows off.

The driver, though invisible
in that dark loft, flies,
by the sound of it,
for cover, screaming

fire or *time*, some irrelevant ordeal
no one aboard would later describe.

PINE CAMP

Frost has peeled scabs of bark from their useless ankles.
Bits of tattered silk hang from their elbows in rags.

Because they have lost their minds
their needles wander off like smoke.

Mushrooms at the base of one trunk
gather like old men for a round and a laugh.

Their holy and beautiful house
is wasting away before their very eyes.

Even the thistle bush out back
gives over, whole, to ice.

All the ivy freezes in motion under the frost.
I'm too young to say this

but mornings like this make me dread my body.
I may wake in fifty years and find it

stamping footprints along the edge of the pines,
trying to inspire terror.

UP IN THE ATTIC WITH THE
ANTIQUE ELECTRIC ORGAN

1.

I come up for the clumsy pleasure
of dusting clean the latticed bench and iron pedal,
to bellow out a few charmed chords
into the insulated sky.

The brass effect of bells makes hollow this cave.
The mildewed lungs rasp like a melancholy stranger.

Even the frantic wasp charging and stunning itself
on the chipped glass of amber bourbon and ice
calms to the sprawling slanted belches of noise.

In this private fiction, the wasp and I
are lone survivors of the snowbound,
frost-shocked deadlock of winter.

Everything we know about agony and the afterlife
is made light of in the glare of this shadeless bulb.

I'm no help to you, wasp. No window to the firmament here.

2.

My brother, whose classic instrument this is,
nailed shut the plaster

the morning of his wedding.
It dawned hot as a rabid lung.

The women heaved up their hems
to fan their varicose thighs while their withered men
wilted in the shadows sucking ice.

He was getting out the only way he knew,
that gaunt blue pain still in his eyes
as he stepped through the place the church doors had shut.

I stayed behind, as if he were my own hope
walking out of me into sunlight,
some invisible cord stretching from his back to my folded hands.

I stayed at the bar drinking laced punch—
it must have been that stinging whiskey
singing in my gut
that jammed my hand through the window
of the locked house I came home to
before the party broke up.

There seemed no other way out of the heat.

The key I forgot was in his suite an hour away,
in the silk suit pocket of his black jacket
thrown haphazard on the bed
as my brother went stark white and naked to the shower.

When I came to the doctor was stitching shut two slashes on my
    wrist,

my sheer, flowered dress scissored off my body.

3.

Another version might imply intention.
Which means we inflict on ourselves the jagged scars.

Another might continue
into the next day, into the diner I worked at,
and the askew style with which I carried the china platters,
too numb in my wrist to feel their weight.

Might include the grease-soaked counter
from which the narcotic customer, seized
by a fit of nerves, rose and flew through the plate-glass window,

a spectacle that put my small drama to shame.

I could still feel it, that strand of clear wire
from my tight hand to his taut body
as I tried to pull him back over to this side.

And the wild sirens arriving
to calm the curious onlookers sidestepping the havoc of blood.

Everything I suspected about relative chance
and the lie of escaping intact
came crashing down to the splattered grass patch I stood on.

The news said he died before any family could locate him
and the medics sent back his laced-up body
to where it came from.

4.

Really, the amateur harmony I'm pumping out now
lives somewhere between

marriage and death, in the narrow zone
between celebration and oblivion, on this electric organ

my brother left behind in the attic,

my brother who calls once a month from his corner
of the skewered planet, my anonymous brother
who sailed through a fever of glass.

He's done our work for us. Therefore,
we'll stay on the stranded border of winter
and play to his memory,

you with the gold ribs of your wings
riddling the air with music,

me on this stained keyboard,

alarmed at our crooked pleasure, at our irresistible pain.

SPRING BLIZZARD

Without warning the calamity of ice closes in
on the first catatonic petals.
By accident he came by today, the man my hand
dreamed up once—
and we were two strangers
balancing in the door frame with a dull porch light
trying to tame the edge of exhaust
speeding by. Like before
he arrived bearing medicine and its curing effects on the body
near death. You could wait forever
said the willow we stood under,
his hand on the storm screen, mine still catching
its breath on another bottle of wine.
But it was already bloody, this scene
lit by daybreak and what passes
over years for exile: one day you start
mistaking loneliness for loveliness, and the branches
weep and freeze. The talk gets tired, the holes in the body
tire. He's going into them,
he tells me, to see what consolation
they might still speak to a self
so ruined. When they sang, when they used to
sing to me, it was snow spindrifting
into what were called angels
fallen in the frozen meadow.
Behind us all the unutterable afternoons
in secret, they get to be a year
and then two and further away

from what anyone in their right mind might figure
worth dying for. Tell me again
what first convinced me.
Tell me how love is a stain on the mind.
Then his tracks in frost leading away,
the rotted hickory nuts like small bombs
firing rounds on the roof that no one hears
for the traffic and distance,
a clay mouth near the window fired open
as if it could swallow what's haunting this air.

ELEMENTS

During those afternoons
you climbed upstairs and into me,
the lilies opened like snow in their valleys,
the snow leaned on my front stoop
like white shoulders.

I think love's gone downriver—
past the sapling lashed to its stake,
past the statue opening its thighs at night—
to sever the ice and rinse
its filthy skeleton.

I should say the crickets' insistence survived.
The moon is still dark and holy
from drowning in the sinkhole under the dam.
On shore, wild swans molt against thistle
and the thistle, by daybreak,
sprouts wings and flies white into white clouds
the snow turns into—
unable to endure burning.

ACKNOWLEDGMENTS

Stephen Mohring, Wendy Gordon, Steve Healey, Kelly Everding, Sean Vernon, Eric Lorberer, Mark Rolo, Hilary Getten, Laura and Mark and Don and Shirley Rawson, Eric Rawson and Callie Cardamon, Kerry O'Keefe: thanks for being with me. Thank you to Arthur Vogelsang, my ideal reader, the Iowa Writers' Workshop and my teachers there, Mark Brumberg and the Globe Bookshop that is no more, the Loft Mentor Series, and the editors and readers of the following journals, in which some of these poems first appeared, several in earlier versions: *The American Poetry Review* ("The Border," "Echo of a Scream," "Flaming June," "Moment's Notice," "Samaritan," "Self-Portraits by Frida Kahlo," "Up in the Attic with the Antique Electric Organ"); *The Antioch Review* ("On Reflection" under the title "Unfinished Piece," "White Nights"); *The Denver Quarterly* ("Diplomatic Imperative"); *Ellipses* ("Willows"); *Passages North* ("After the Riots," "Phantom Pain"); *The Taos Review* ("American Incident," "Border Camp," "Spring Blizzard").

Joanna Rawson was born in Kansas and raised in Iowa. She earned her M.F.A. at the Iowa Writers' Workshop and has since published poems, essays, and articles in the *American Poetry Review*, the *Denver Quarterly*, *Salon*, and other magazines. She lives in Minneapolis.